Freeman Delamotte

A Primer of The Art of Illumination for the Use of Beginners

With a rudimentary treatise on the art, practical directionsfor its exercise, and

examples taken from illuminated mss.

Freeman Delamotte

A Primer of The Art of Illumination for the Use of Beginners
With a rudimentary treatise on the art, practical directionsfor its exercise, and examples taken from illuminated mss.

ISBN/EAN: 9783337625108

Printed in Europe, USA, Canada, Australia, Japan

Cover: Foto ©Thomas Meinert / pixelio.de

More available books at **www.hansebooks.com**

A PRIMER OF
The Art of Illumination

For the Use of Beginners;

WITH
A RUDIMENTARY TREATISE ON THE ART, PRACTICAL DIRECTIONS
FOR
ITS EXERCISE, AND EXAMPLES TAKEN FROM ILLUMINATED MSS.

BY

F. DELAMOTTE.

London:—E. & F. N. SPON,
16, BUCKLERSBURY.

1860.

LONDON:
PRINTED BY BOWLES AND SONS,
GEORGE STREET, MANSION HOUSE, E.C.

Contents.

Outlines of the above

xiii. to xx.

Preface.

As the taste for illumination continues to spread, the want of an elementary work on the art becomes more and more keenly felt. Persons possessed of real artistic skill turn their attention to it, and after designing and executing work which, according to all the rules of art known to them, ought to produce a correct and pleasing result, are amazed at the ungainly conglomeration which is the reward of their labour. The secret of this is, they are unacquainted with the fundamental principles of the art. Others, setting to work in a safer way, place before them a specimen of mediæval illuminating work, and endeavour to produce an accurate copy of it; they too are amazed at finding that, after all the pains bestowed on it, their copy has an effect so different from that of the original. The secret of this is, they are unacquainted with the peculiar method of manipulating the colours, &c. used in illuminating. What both need is, elementary instruction in—first—the principles; and, secondly—the practice of the art.

It is to supply this want that the 'PRIMER OF ILLUMINATION' has been conceived. It contains just so much instruction on the history and principles of the art, as may serve to fix on certain definite bases, the wandering and somewhat hazy notions of people on the subject, and enable them, by reference to good examples, to erect their own superstructure on a certain foundation; and just so much instruction in the practical part of the art as may enable them, in a great measure, to teach themselves how to practise it. Advice is also given on the selection and purchase of colours, instruments, &c., and a progressive set of studies, printed both in outline and in the proper colours, and gold, is added to furnish models for copying.

Incidentally, an effort has been made to correct a few of the prevalent popular errors on the subject—such, for instance, as that every illuminated service book is a 'missal,' and so forth—and which errors stand sorely in the way of the beginner's right comprehension of the subject.

All the examples selected have been taken from undoubted authorities, and will be recognized by persons acquainted with mediæval books.

Part I.

In a work of a merely practical character anything like a critical or historical dissertation on the art of illumination would of course be out of place. The growing or rather reviving taste in this and neighbouring countries which has during the last twenty or thirty years brought to light such vast treasures of mediæval art, which had lain for three centuries buried under a heap of pseudo-classical rubbish, has elicited amongst its most pleasing features a host of works on illumination which, without exhausting a subject which is inexhaustible, have at least contributed largely to place this beautiful art on its proper pedestal, and investigate and develope the rules by which it is governed. These works are of course of different pretensions and varying beauty, though of the majority it may fairly be alleged that they are magnificent and brilliant specimens of typography, and that the research and ability displayed in their contents are fully equal to the beauty of their illustrations. From such works the history of the rise and progress, the culmination and decadence of the art may be easily traced, and a catena of characteristics constructed. The principal defect exhibited by almost all these works is that their (necessarily) large price places them out of the reach of all but the wealthy, and it may be added that even when access can be obtained to them they are found to contain no practical directions for cultivating and practising the art of which they treat.

It is the object of this little work to supply this deficiency, to place within every one's reach just the sort of information and instruction which a master might be supposed to give his pupil, and to enable persons with a taste for illuminating to answer for themselves the universally-asked question, "How am I to set about it?"

What illumination really is, or rather what is and what is not illumination, in the strict sense of the word, it is not so easy to define as might be supposed. Define it as ornamental letter writing; but every ornamental letter is not necessarily an illuminated one—witness our shop fronts for instance. Illumination is extending, it is true, to them, and has been employed in some instances with marked success: but a mere tyro can select two specimens, and say without a moment's hesitation which is and which is not illumination, and yet it would puzzle an experienced illuminator to define logically the difference. It is not however so material to hunt for definitions, as by acquaintance and experience to acquire such a general knowledge of its leading characteristics as will enable the mind to arrive at that by instinct, which it is difficult to do by definition. For most purposes it may perhaps suffice to define it as a peculiar system of ornamenting manuscript or letterpress, which leaves the body of the matter intact, or only fills up the *hiatus* at the ends of paragraphs, bestows on the initial letter or letters an ornamentation more or less elaborate and profuse, extends that ornamentation along the top and down the left side of the matter, or still further extending, envelopes the whole in a sort of framework of colour, gilding, &c. This description will do for addresses, charters, scroll work and the like, as well as for what have ever afforded the greatest scope for illumination—books.[1]

It has been announced already that there is no intention of introducing into this work a dissertation on the history of illumination. It is however essential to the successful study of the art, even in its most moderate form, to obtain some general notion of its rise and progress, and of the sort of works, and of what dates to look into, for the best and most characteristic specimens. In furnishing a key to this portion of the study, we propose to avail ourselves, by way of illustration, of specimens, accessible to all without charge, namely, those displayed in the glass cases of the king's library, and adjoining manuscript saloon at the British Museum.

Where, when, and how the idea of ornamenting writings first sprung into existence, is as immaterial as it is difficult to discover. It is the fashion to ascribe its origin, in common with that of many other arts and sciences, to the East; and indeed, the presence at the Museum of several beautiful specimens of oriental illuminated MSS. would appear to denote a very high condition of the art in Persia and Hindostan at an early date; but in reality it is not improbable that the art was springing into existence simultaneously, or nearly so, in several parts of the world at once. The styles of the oriental illumination already alluded to, of the ancient Byzantine, of the early Roman, and the Hibernian, are fundamentally dissimilar, and probably came into existence independently of each other. It is from the last-named country—Ireland—then far in advance of all neighbouring lands in civilization and learning, that it seems most probable England first received the art. History informs us of what was done for the then inhabitants of this country by missionary monks from the island of St. Patrick, and there can be no doubt they would bring their service books, or at least the art of writing them, along with them, and so spread the knowledge of their art side by side with that of their religion; and it is remarkable that one of the earliest, if not the earliest specimens of the art of illumination extant in this country, is a copy of the Gospels made for Macbrid Mac Dernan, in (as is supposed) the year

885, and now to be found in the library at Lambeth Palace. The style of this very early age of the art is quaint but highly characteristic. It shares with the Byzantine a severity and simplicity of outline, and an intricacy of interlacing in the details, which are very striking—one specimen in our first page of examples, it may be added, is taken from this curious work.

Once in England the Hibernian element would naturally meet, mingle with, and finally be absorbed in the ever-progressing and improving tide of taste setting in from the Continent, or spontaneously springing out of the varying developments of art and science in England itself. We are not therefore surprised to find—and this must ever be borne in mind—that the science of architecture and the sister arts of illuminating, metal working, wood carving, embroidery, and perhaps we may add fresco painting, passed on hand in hand through a nearly parallel course of development through the middle ages, all culminating together, as far as chasteness of design and elegance of execution were concerned, in the 13th and 14th centuries, and as far as profuseness and richness of ornamentation were concerned, in the 15th; and all together sinking out of sight during the Reformation. And the reason why, in obtaining a general view of the progress of one—as illumination—it is wise to keep the others in mind, is, that each serves, and especially architecture as a sort of *memoria technica* to the rest. Thus whilst the severe straight lines and semicircles of the Norman school prevail, a corresponding simplicity of outline characterizes the illuminations of the period; the same grotesque lizard-shaped monsters, which twine themselves round the capitals of the columns form the components or terminals of the initials in the service books; and even a resemblance may be traced between, at least, one kind of beading and the exterior ornamentation of the writing. When the graceful and luxuriant curves of foliage begin to steal into the pages of the MS. they are to be found also forming the capital of the column, though here it must be confessed the former somewhat outruns the latter—a style of illumination generally known as the *opus Anglicum*, and claimed as the peculiar invention of this country, having been in use more than a century before the foliage, which is one of its characteristics, appears in the capital. Further on, when flowers are added to foliage in the one, they appear in the other; when the angular principle is introduced into architecture, it shews itself in illumination; and when outline is in the one almost buried under prodigal elaboration of detail, the other seems to have all the riches, animal as well as vegetable, of the park and the flower garden, poured over its pages to smother the text.

The leading characteristics of the different principles of illumination, as developed during an investigation into specimens, of the changes successively introduced as above, will be found to be—

1st.—The component parts of the initial itself are made the subject of ornamentation; sometimes by the contortion of a dragon or some other pliable animal into a grotesque parody of the shape of the letter; sometimes by forming it of a combination of geometric figures, resulting from an endless crossing of lines, the whole terminating in heads or other parts of the same sort of creatures; sometimes by the introduction of foliage in a more or less integral manner.

2nd.—The ornamentation oozing over as it were beyond the limits of the letter itself, extends in a straggling manner upwards and downwards, or downwards and along, forming a partial fringe to the corner or margin of the page.

3rd.—The initial regains its simplicity of outline, but is laid upon a cartouche of ornamental work or of diaper work, the species of ornamentation mentioned in No. 2 being nearly detached from the letter, and forming a kind of canopy—or, as it is customary to call it 'bracket'—over it.

4th.—The bracket is extended all round the page, and becomes an illuminated border. Illustrations, such as scenes, portraits, &c. are introduced within. The initial dwindles, as does the space for the text, which frequently occupies but a tiny islet, in the midst of a sea of rich decoration.

The whole of these resolve themselves into two leading principles: the one where the initial itself is the illumination, and its outline and component parts are the subject of treatment. The other, where the initial remains in its simplicity of outline, and the ornamentation is bestowed on what surrounds it, or on that on which it is imposed.

Our list of examples from the British Museum will be found to contain specimens of nearly all the different styles we have alluded to, and to display most of the leading characteristics. It is hardly necessary to add, that there are vast treasures of this art lying at the same place, and to be got at with a little trouble, and from these it would have been easy enough to have selected some more favourable specimens of some of the styles; and it is to be hoped that a larger proportion of these treasures, than the somewhat meagre allowance at present placed within the reach of the general public may some day be made generally accessible. In this work, for the reason already stated, nothing has been included which is not open to all the world to inspect. It should further be prefaced that the Italian specimens have been placed by themselves, partly because the majority of them belong to a different school, in which the classical element naturally introduces itself to a greater or less extent, and partly because they well deserve a distinct examination, being in general far more richly executed than the others,

(and they belong besides all to one period, the latter half of the 15th and the very beginning of the 16th century.)

No distinction has been made between MS. and printed works in the selection, because the large majority of the illuminations in the latter—amounting in our selection to all but one—are done by hand, and are therefore quite as useful by way of study as if they appeared on the most undoubted vellum MS. that had ever borne the scrutiny of all the archæologists. Separate mention also is made of the Oriental illuminations.

It is perhaps hardly necessary to add that nearly all the specimens will be found to have been taken from books, for the simple reason that by far the larger proportion of all mediæval illumination was bestowed upon them: of these it is not surprising to find Ecclesiastical works coming in for the largest share of attention. The service books in use in mediæval days,[2] in churches and cathedrals, were numerous; and being, as to a large part of their contents, accompanied by the old musical notation, executed in a large bold type, were necessarily of considerable size; indeed, as a general rule, about that of our modern music paper, that is, rather larger than the prayer books generally in use in our cathedrals in these days. Of these service books some of the principal were—the Missal or Mass book, the Lectionary, which contained the lessons for each day, the Psalter, the Hymnarium or book of hymns, the Antiphonarium or anthem book: these were in constant daily use, and there were besides a number of other books containing offices, benedictions, &c. for special occasions. The book of private devotion, in use among the laity, was called the book of Hours, as it contained prayers, psalms, &c. for all the canonical hours during the day; and for the clergy and religious, there was the Breviary as well. The above list will convey but a meagre notion of the number and variety of the books in use in the middle ages, in connexion with the service of the church. It may be added, by the way, that the libraries of cathedrals, monasteries, and religious houses were well furnished with copies of the Gospels, and of the other books composing the sacred volume; of which, occasionally, also copies found their way into the comparatively small collections of great men. From the above sketch, however, it may be gathered, what a field was afforded, by this variety of books, for the exercise of the art under consideration. The large vellum sheets on which the various offices were to be inscribed must have been a source of almost revelry to the imaginations of such members of the monastic institution, always in those days attached to a cathedral, as were the fortunate possessors of artistic taste; and it is probable that, to the monastic body, the work of illumination was always generally, and through all the earlier centuries exclusively, confided. It was not until it began to assume a place as a recognized art, in all probability, that regular professors and practisers of it sprung up outside the walls of the monastery;[3] but however and by whomsoever practised, there was always plenty to be done—besides the regular business of replacing, perpetuating, and increasing the contents of the cathedral or monastic library—there were always great and wealthy men, desirous of possessing for themselves, or of presenting to their friends or patrons, such books as a copy of the Gospels, or, more generally, a book of Hours; and the richness and magnificence of the work executed, would bear a sort of exact proportion to the liberality of the customer, or the greatness of the destined owner. It was in this way that such splendid works came into existence, as the Gospels made for Macbrid Mac Dernan, already mentioned; the Lectionary presented by Lord Lovell to the church of Salisbury; the celebrated Hours of Anne of Brittany, generally understood to have been presented to her by

Louis XII; those of S. Louis, of Henry VII., of the Duke of Anjou, of Queen Mary; the great Hours of the Duke of Berri; the golden Gospels; the Bibles written for Charlemagne, for Charles the Bald; and a host of other magnificent works which, at this day, supply those specimens of the art which modern illuminators take for their models, and occupy, in relation to it, the same place as the old masters' pictures to painting, and the temples of Greece and Rome, and the cathedrals of England and France, to architecture.

But the art of illumination, though principally employed on works connected with the services of the church, or with private devotion, was far from being exclusively so occupied. Chronicles and histories, and descriptions and travels, as well as poems and other compositions, and the classics, all received more or less ornamentation, according to the same rule of proportion already laid down for service books, and books of hours. Dedications were common; and what we should now call a presentation copy, was frequently adorned with magnificent illustration, in honour of the great man under whose auspices the work issued, and of whom it was not unusual to introduce a portrait into the title or first page, representing him 'as he appeared' receiving the presentation copy from the author. Of this kind are the Recollation of the Chronicles of England written for Edward the IV., 1460; Capgrave's Commentary on Genesis, dedicated to Humphrey Duke of Gloucester, 1438; Old Mandeville's Wonders of the World, 14th century; Lydgate's poem, or rather translation of the Pelerinage de l'Homme, dedicated to the great Earl of Warwick, 1430; and many others. Of the classics many beautiful editions have come down to us, both in MS. and printed, illuminated with exquisite taste—the classic element being very naturally introduced more liberally here than into the books of religion, or even of local interest. The 15th century is rich in such works; and Italy, as might be supposed, produces the best. The King's Library, at the British Museum, displays more, in proportion, of these specimens of the art than of any other; and many of them will repay careful study for the sake of their extreme chasteness, the excellence of their taste, and the comprehensiveness of their general arrangement.

It may be readily conjectured that books thus produced were exceedingly valuable; indeed, every one is aware what a serious and palpable effect the price of books, before the introduction and development of the art of printing, exercised on the spread of literature; and though it was not every copy of every work that was made the subject of those brilliant appliances of red, and blue, and gold, which glitter on the leaves open beneath the glass cases at the Museum, yet even ordinary and less pretentious works received some sort of simple ornamentation, principally in the shape of giving the initial letters of chapters or paragraphs in colour, filling up the vacant spaces at the end of either with a simple outline flourish, somewhat resembling the earlier Greek borders, introducing red lines between the written ones, and in general—to use a very familiar phrase—'smartening up' the appearance of the work. When, however, the artist and the skilled workman were called in to exert their energies, and exercise their ingenuity on the more magnificent, both of course had to be remunerated, in proportion to the prominence of their part in the production of the work, and the value of their labour naturally entered largely as an almost principal item into the heavy prices paid for such books: it may be added, however, that the cost of binding formed generally an almost equally extravagant item in the calculation, to understand which, it will merely be necessary to look into one or two of the cases, in the rooms we have referred to, specially devoted to specimens of magnificent binding. Under these circumstances the value of illuminated books need be no longer a wonder. We select, however, one instance by way of closing this digression. The same Duke Humphrey, of whom mention has already been made, presented in the year 1440, to the University of Oxford, a collection of some 600 volumes, among which there were 120 which were valued alone at 1,000*l.*, between 1,800*l.* and 1,900*l.* of our present money.[4] They were the most splendid and costly copies that could be procured, finely written on vellum, and elegantly embellished with miniatures and illuminations. The narrator feelingly deplores, by the way, the utter destruction or removal of all this magnificent donation, with the single exception of a copy of a Valerius Maximus, by the pious visitors of the University, in the reign of Edward VI., whose zeal was only equalled by their ignorance, or perhaps by their avarice; because these books, being highly ornamented, looked like missals. It will be scarcely necessary to remind the reader that the treasures of the art of illumination in this country suffered—besides the weeding out of the Reformation—a second grand onslaught in the succeeding century, when the troopers of the Commonwealth tore up and scattered to the winds the beautiful contents of many a nobleman's and private gentleman's library, from the precisely similar reason that they were full of popish pictures. The first raid was on the ecclesiastical, the second on the lay libraries; and that so many treasures of art escaped, is probably owing to the circumstance, that the more intelligent and provident, both of churchmen and laymen—and let it be added those amongst both who appreciated their books as highly, or more so, than their plate—concealed them in cellars and out of the way places, before the storm fell on them. On the whole, it would seem as though England has suffered in this matter more than any other country, from the indiscriminating fury of bigotted fanatics.

Another class of subjects of the art to which allusion has already been made, consists of official documents, such as charters, grants, diplomas, &c., the dignity of which it appears to have been not unusual to enhance by the aid of ornamentation. As far as can be gathered, however, the custom seems to have obtained more in Italy than in this country; and it is only mentioned here, partly as exhibiting a distinct department of the art, and partly because one of the most striking specimens, to which reference will be made, is a grant by a Duke of Milan to his wife, of lands in the territories of Novara Pavia and Milan, (1494,) and which for beauty of conception, excellence of execution, and above all chasteness of tone, has not its equal among all the specimens adduced. Such a grant is a sort of counterpart to our marriage settlement; but this may be the best place to warn beginners not to confound law engrossing with illumination. The former is—or was, and might again become—a beautiful art of itself; some magnificent specimens of it exist—the charter of the law society for one—but the arts are distinct and the characters different. The only work in which the two frequently meet in these days, and present in that combination a very fair reproduction, by the way, of these very charters and diplomas of which we are now treating, is the engrossment of those singularly worded documents in which a public body is wont to inform an exalted personage, that they "beg to approach her with the profoundest, &c., &c., &c.," in short, of an address.

There yet remains to mention another department of the art, which during the last few years has become a very favourite and somewhat popular vehicle for its revival and development. This is what is generally known as "scroll work," under which head, though the title is strictly applicable to but one sort, it is proposed to include, for convenience' sake, all sorts of writing on, or attached to walls. The growth of this department of the art may be easily traced in connexion with the growth of intelligence and learning generally. In days when few besides ecclesiastics could read, it was a very obvious mode of instruction—akin to what goes on now in the nursery and the infant school—to cover interior walls, and especially those of churches, with pictures, illustrating, either by actual historical events or in allegory, those moral and religious lessons which it was desired to inculcate; and many such fresco paintings, as they are curiously enough called, have recently come to light from under the coats of whitewash with which modern economy had carefully covered them up—and though this method of instruction, through the medium of wall painting, never quite died out, and has been the subject of a noble resuscitation in these days, yet it was again obviously natural that, as people more generally acquired the power of reading, and as, simultaneously, a feeling against any sort of figures inside churches—always except the lion and unicorn of the Caroline days—sprung up, those lessons which had hitherto been pictorially should now be directly inculcated; in short, that the picture book should be laid aside for the grammar. There came to help a canon, ordering the setting up of the Lord's Prayer, Creed, and Ten Commandments, and thus by degrees texts of scripture came to appear along the string courses, following the spring of the arches, or adorning the side walls, &c. Modern architects have availed themselves largely of this custom; and in many modern churches, not only are texts introduced as features in the architecture, but also in quaintly-devised scrolls along the walls, whilst the Creed, &c. have been made the vehicle of elaborate ornamentation at the east end.

That most of these instructive adornments of the walls of churches, schools, &c. are painted on the wall itself, and so in a manner are taken out of the category of the art which is the peculiar subject of this work, by no means deprives them of a place in it altogether, for they are all as truly specimens and products of the art as what is executed on vellum or cardboard, only bearing to the latter about the same relation as fresco painting does to the canvas picture.

At Christmas time particularly, as well as on some other festive occasions, it is not unusual to see an almost indefinite multiplication of this scroll work executed on paper or cardboard, and sometimes in embroidery, affixed temporarily to the walls. Of these temporary decorations, which generally exhibit strong internal evidence of their being the work of beginners, it would be illnatured to say more than that they are specimens rather of hearty zeal than of good taste, and that a rudimentary acquaintance, even, with mediæval examples, might have saved them from inflicting pain on critical eyes, whilst they would have been equally the admiration of the uninitiated.

A remarkable instance of this department of the art, and one not unworthy of imitation, is to be found mentioned in the 'Expenses of Louis XI,' in which a sum is entered as paid to one 'Bourdichon, painter and illuminator,' for having executed in 'Azure fifty large scrolls,' which the king had caused to be set up in several places in Plessis du Parc, and on which was written, *Misericordias Domini in æternum Cantabo,* (I will sing the mercies of the Lord for ever;) and 'for having painted and pourtrayed in gold and Azure,—and other colours, three angels, three feet high or thereabouts, each of which holds one of these scrolls in his hand, and appears to be writing the aforesaid *Misericordia.'*

This part of the subject must not be entirely abandoned without a passing mention of what may, at first sight, appear hardly to form a legitimate department of the art, but which even a cursory examination of mediæval illuminated work will shew to have formed an integral and prominent feature in it, and to be therefore fairly reckoned as a distinct section of it. This is the Monogram[5] —the most ancient of all ornamentation used in Christendom. For on the walls of those catacombs, into which the persecuted Christians of the earlier centuries of the Church's history at Rome descended to celebrate their devotions and bury their dead, and the long unknown treasures of which are still being brought to light, the same or nearly the same sacred monogram is frequently to be met with, as appears curiously twisted into the brilliant initiatory pages of the earlier illuminated books, and a poor imitation of which is still to be seen adorning the front of many a red velvet altar cloth in our English churches at this day. The use of the monogram, however, was far more extended than this. In mediæval times, almost every prince and great man had the initial letters of his name woven into a monogram or device, which appeared in his books, on his housings, on the badges of his domestics, in the architecture of his palace—everywhere, in short, where it could form a feature of ornament. Later on, the early printers each adopted one, and the practice has been thus gradually handed down to our days, when the use of them is becoming almost universal. It is a pretty and ingenious department of the art, but requires some study of good models in order to arrive at its principles, and prevent quaintness from degenerating into clumsiness or absurdity.

In furnishing the beginner with some clue to the best styles for study, there is considerable difficulty, arising from *l'embarras des richesses*. One of the best modern authorities on the art enumerates no less than nine successive styles, exclusive of the Italian, all of which, with a single exception, present distinct features of beauty; and the larger work, by the same author, presents three times that number of specimens. From such a mass of materials as this, elimination is not easy. Nevertheless, for all the purposes of this elementary work, it need only be necessary to enumerate four leading styles for study, leaving for any future and more advanced work the filling up of the interstices between these four, and the more expanded description of all.

The First may be referred to the earliest centuries of the introduction of the art into this country, perhaps from the 6th to the 9th; its leading characteristics, which are rather distinguished by quaintness than beauty, have been well described as 'an artistic and ingenious disposition of interwoven threads, bands, or ribbons, of various colours, upon black or coloured grounds, varied by the introduction of extremely attenuated lizard-like reptiles, birds, and other animals, similarly treated.[6] The initials are frequently of enormous size, and extreme intricacy.' A frequent peculiarity is the practice of surrounding all external outlines with rows of minute red dots.

The Second belongs to the 10th and 11th centuries, and has been already alluded to as the *opus Anglicum*. The general characteristics are, a border to the whole text, constructed of parallel stripes, or bars of gold, between and around which a style of foliage, in perfect harmony with the solidity of the framework, intertwines itself in a graceful and quite peculiar manner.[7]

The Third may be referred generally to the 14th century, when, as has been before remarked, the art reached its culminating point, as far as chasteness of design and elegance of execution were concerned. The period has been well denominated 'a great artistic era, when the architecture, the painting, the goldsmith's work, the elaborate productions in enamel, and the illuminator's art, were all in beautiful harmony, being each founded on similar principles of design and composition.' It is not easy to lay down any but a few leading characteristics, as the specimens are as varied in construction as they are in the style of their beauty. One leading feature however is, the profuse use of what are technically called 'ivy leaves,' as an accessory to borders and initials, and which, tastefully handled, produce very much the effect of filagree work;[8] miniatures and miniature scenes, coats of arms, &c., are introduced at the corners of the page, and at proper intervals along the frame border; tiny birds of gay plumage are perched here and there among the foliage; and the conventional acanthus begins to be associated with natural flowers, &c., leading the way to—

The Fourth style, or that in which richness and profuseness of decoration reached their culminating point. The end of the 15th and beginning of the 16th centuries may claim this style of which—though as of the last, it may be truly said the varieties are countless—the leading characteristic is the solid border; by which is meant that the foliage, flowers, birds, animals, &c., which hitherto formed an open border with no background, are now as it were strewed about upon a carpet of gold, or of some good background colour, the effect being heightened by the introduction of shading to 'throw up' the objects pourtrayed.[9]

The Italian style of the 15th century to which alone reference will be here made, is characterised more or less by all the peculiar beauties of the third and fourth styles just described, but, as might have been expected, with a strong admixture of the classical element both in outline, foliage and general treatment; in fact, it may be described as consisting of these two styles cast in a classical mould.

There is one species of illumination chiefly applicable to initials, quite unique in its exquisite chasteness, for which we are indebted to Italy. It consists of interlacing branches, quite white, laid upon a parti-coloured floor, the effect being that a different colour appears through every adjoining interstice of the branches. The background is frequently lightened by being strewed over with white dots.

The Oriental style of illumination is principally characterised by a profuse use of filagree work and gold, and by the introduction of numerous exquisitely-finished miniatures and miniature pictures, in which it is not uncommon to find the faces drawn on tiny disks of ivory, and attached to the page *in situ*.

Of the character employed in executing the text of an illuminated piece of work, it may suffice to point out—first, that it should agree chronologically with the style of illumination adopted; next, that it should harmonize with it in an artistic point of view; and thirdly, that simple styles of character are preferable.[10]

The object of this introductory sketch being rather to lay down general principles, leaving the student to work them out than to follow him through the whole study, for which, indeed, there is no space, it may be as well, in the first instance, to point out the two leading errors into which modern illuminators are apt to fall. The one is a slavish imitation of mediæval models; the other, the unrestrained indulgence of the illuminator's own fancy. Both are vicious, though the latter far more so than the former—for the mediæval illuminators had real taste and artistic feeling; and the modern copyist, by his slavish reproduction, unconsciously appropriates to himself what they possessed; while the other, wandering about in the uncultivated wilderness of his own ideas, picks up and piles together a mass of incongruous materials—of which, when he has completed the extraordinary jumble, he cannot in the least comprehend why the result is so unsatisfactory. But the fact is, illumination (like every other art) has its grammar, and that grammar lies in the mediæval books; but when the grammar is mastered, there is no reason why modern intelligence should not be emancipated from the trammels of everything but its fundamental principles.

The principle of the construction of a border, in the style of the celebrated Hours of Anne of Brittany, may be strictly adhered to, for instance; but the details and their treatment may be quite new. Nor because the figures introduced into an Anglo-Saxon illuminated bible are generally dislocated about the hips, and display a tendency to postures of the feet, impossible even to the most flexible dancer, is it necessary to reproduce in a modern illumination of the same style the same unnatural distortions.

And these remarks lead naturally to another, namely, that some study of the principles of the harmonies of outline, of form, and above all of colour, is essential to the successful study of the art of illumination.

Nor will anything more materially promote this study than a careful consideration of the harmonies enumerated, as they are exhibited in nature, both animal and vegetable, but particularly the latter, as something of a bower seems the fundamental idea of all the better styles of the art. All sorts of creeping plants, whether in the garden or the hedgerow; all sorts of flowers, exotic, native, or wild—nay, fruits and many vegetables—as parsley, notably—may be pressed with advantage into the service of the art: whilst the graceful forms and beautiful plumage of the bird tribe, especially of the inhabitants of the Tropics; the equally brilliant though more delicate plumage of butterflies and moths; the symmetrical contour and tasteful combinations of colour in many quadrupeds; and even the homelier insects which crawl about our fruit trees, may be all studied with advantage. The old illuminators were frequently happy to avail themselves of a caterpillar, or a lady bird, to break the monotony of a broad, flat space, or heighten the effect of a leaf, or balance a too obtrusive colour in an opposite corner. Reptiles, too, may contribute much that is exceedingly beautiful, both in outline and colour; and in this respect again the Tropics furnish the most brilliant specimens.

Besides the book of nature itself, then, all sorts of works (with coloured illustrations) on Botany and Zoology, may with advantage be consulted; nor need Conchology be disregarded: some of the more beautiful shells forming admirable subjects of study for the illuminator. And where books are inaccessible, there is at any rate the department of Natural History, at the British Museum, open to every one.

Lastly, it will be useful to take every opportunity of marking how other arts have treated the same subjects— Architecture and Metal working particularly. Such observations will tend to shew above all how the principle and idea of the natural may be translated into the conventional, without loss of grace. The carvings in the capitals of some of the early English columns supply the best instances.

For these last purposes the mediæval courts of the Crystal Palace may be made excellent schools—as the Alhambra court, for the study of colour in its richest combinations. The Kensington Museum might form a general school for both.

We proceed next to furnish a catalogue of those specimens at the British Museum which are best calculated to assist the beginner in his studies.

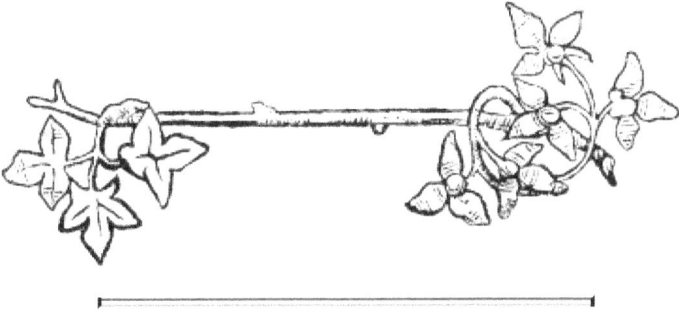

English and French Specimens.

DATE.	NAME OF SPECIMEN.	POINTS TO BE NOTED.	WHE[...] BE FO[...]
9th cent.	Latin bible, written on vellum, according to the Vulgate, as revised by Alcuin.	Character of initials displaying the first principle mentioned.	MS. S[...] upr[...] Case[...]
12th cent.	A volume of a Latin bible written for the monastery at Arnstein.	Initial letters, "In Principio," covering entire page, and interlaced.	D[...] Case l[...]
Abt. 1300	The Books of the Maccabees.	Arrangement of illustrations, in rows of medallions— displays little or no principle— but is curious.	D[...] Case[...] compa[...] (D[...]
End 14th or beginning of	Fragment of a Lectionary written for Lord Lovell,	This is a brilliant specimen, though it has	D[...] 6[...] compa[...] (H[...]

15th cent.	and presented by him to Salisbury.	been maltreated. Observe the framework or border—the filagree work—ivy leaves—miniature scene illustrative—coatsof arms introduced, &c.	
1493.	Les Chroniques de France.	All are well worth studying, for the beauty of the borders, as well as for general arrangement.	Kir Libı Cas
1493 and 1498.	Hours for the use of the diocese of Rome (Paris.) —Pigouchet		
1493	L'Art et Science de Rhetorique (Paris.)	A good specimen of the counterchanged border.	D Case
1470	Justinus's Abridgement of Trogus	Borders and Initials.	D Cas
1471	Fichet— Rhetoricorum libri.		D Cas

Italian and German Specimens.

[In the three first specimens selected, an instance will be observed of a species of ornamentation to which the name of 'pottering' has been familiarly applied; it consists of a sort of fringe to the initial and part of the text, resembling in arrangement the 'bracket,' and in principle the flourishes of a modern writing master; but when tastefully applied, it is remarkably effective, and has the advantage of being very easy.]

DATE.	NAME OF SPECIMEN.	POINTS TO BE NOTED.	WHERE TO BE FOUND.	
1455.	The Mazarine Bible.	Initial, red and white.	Case III.	1
1457.	The Mentz Psalter.	Initial and border.	Do.	3
1459.	Do. (2nd edition)	Do.	Do.	4
1462.	Bible in Latin.	A peculiar and bold kind of initial.	Do.	5
1469.	Livy.	The white branch on parti-	Case VI.	2

		coloured ground.		
"	Cicero, Tusculanæ Questiones.	Initial and bracket.	Do.	3
"	Cicero, Epistolæ familiares.	The white branch, &c.	Do.	10
1470.	Cicero, Epistolæ, &c.	Border and initial.	Do.	10
1480.	Æsop's Fables.	Border.	Do.	8
1481.	Liber Psalmorum.	Border.	Do.	9
1482.	Euclid's Geometry.	The white branch, on parti-coloured background.	Case X.	5
1484.	Breviary of the Camaldolese Monks.	Border and initials.	Case IX.	1
1501.	Martial— Epigrammata.	Border and picture.	Case X.	7
1513.	Aulus Gellius —Noctes Atticæ.	Border.	Do.	19
1514.	Plautus— Comedies.	Border, &c.	Do.	20

Specimen of a Grant (Italian.)

1494.	Ludovico Maria Sforza Visconti, Duke of Milan, to his wife.	The ornamental work which occupies the whole upper part of this specimen is worthy of minute and careful study. It is magnificent.	Miscellaneous Autographs, &c.

Oriental Specimens.

DATE.	NAME OF SPECIMEN.	POINTS TO BE NOTED.	WHERE TO BE FOUND.
	The Sri Bhagavat Purana.	Miniature pictures, set in borders— illuminated framework- gilding.	Central table Case 1st compartment 4
	The Durga- patha. A Bhuddistic work and Hindoo miniatures.	Do.	Do. 3rd compartment 23 and 24
1305.	A volume containing the Koran.	Illuminated borders— use of gold.	Side Case, IV. (D.)
16th cent.	Khizr Khan.	Miniature scenes and border.	Central table Case 4th compartment 3
17th cent.	The Diwan (Háfiz).	Do.	Do. 3

There are also some beautiful specimens to be seen at the Mu

East India House.

Part II.

1º *Paper.—*

Several obvious reasons combined in mediæval days to make vellum the almost exclusive vehicle for illuminated writing. It was the substance on which most manuscript books were written: it was durable, and it took both ink and colour well. It is still largely in use for the purposes of illumination, and may be had properly prepared at almost any stationer's, as well as at all artists' colour shops. Any drawing paper with a smooth surface may also be used; but the best substance of all is the ordinary Bristol board, not too thick, for there should be some little elasticity—three sheets thick is about the most useful.

2º *Colours.—*

So much in illumination depends on (1º) the brilliancy and (2º) the durability of the colours employed, that too much care can hardly be displayed in their selection. Instances are numerous in which work on which hours and hours of care and pains were bestowed, a few years ago, is now so faded as to be almost unintelligible; the reds have flown, the whites turned brown, and a few hazy, blue marks are all that are left. It is clear that they of old surpassed us in the preparation of their colours. Some of the paintings in the ancient temples of Egypt, which have been proved to be only water colour, are as brilliant and fresh to-day as they were when laid on three thousand years ago. The exquisite miniatures and elaborate ornamentation of numbers of Oriental manuscripts, five, six, seven, and more centuries old, retain all their original beauty and gorgeousness; and the mediæval office books, and other MSS. of England, France, and Italy, especially those of the 14th century, are at this day as much marvels of brilliant colouring as the stained glass windows of the same periods. To the beginner, of course, the character of the colours employed is not so important, as to more forward artists. Still it is wise to exercise judgment in selection, even from the first, especially as in nine cases out of ten a cake of colour will last for years. The best course is to make the purchases at one of the best artists' colour shops, to eschew all 'made up' colours, and to rely on the eye for producing at home the several gradations of hue, by mixing the primal colours on the slab. Comparatively few are really required; and as illuminating is a very different art from ordinary water-colour drawing, and requires a peculiar texture of matter, the colours most fitted for it are not always the same as those in ordinary use. The following will be found the most serviceable:—

REDS.	YELLOWS & BROWNS.	SILVERS.
Scarlet vermillion	Indian yellow	The most durable mode
Crimson vermillion	Gamboge	of producing this most
Crimson lake	Sepia	delicate and sensitive
Carmine	The latter, mixed with	of all colours, is to
The two last for	lake, makes a good	use platina, or

the deeper hues, and for shading.

BLUES.

Ultramarine

Permanent blue

The latter for the

deeper hues, and

for shading.

NEUTRAL TINTS, PURPLES, &c.

Permanent blue, mixed with

shadow colour, and shows well on reds, or on gold.

BLACKS.

Indian ink

This will be found the most generally useful. Ivory black and lamp black are both good blacks; but genuine Indian ink is as good, or better, and has the advantage of working well in the pen, which the others will not do.

GREENS.

Emerald green—

aluminum, and burnish

afterwards.

See 'Tricks.'

WHITES.

Chinese white is the most brilliant and stands best.

GOLDS.

The ordinary shell

lake, will be found best suited for illumination. The neutral tint sold in the shops is too heavy, so is that ordinarily made up of indigo and light red.

for the shading.

be found most economical to purchase it in the larger quantities, as sold in Porcelain pans and saucers. There is also a gold medium, the use of which as well as of the agate burnisher, will be explained under the head of 'Tricks.'

Pencils, Pens, Drawing Instruments, &c.

The pencil being only used for sketching the subjects, those marked F, H, and HH, will be found sufficient. A few ordinary fine-pointed steel pens will do very well for outlining. For the benefit of any learner not conversant with the use of the pen with colour, it may be added that the method is, to mix the colour, very liquid, in a saucer; and then filling a camel's hair brush with some, to draw the brush across the shoulder of the pen, which is to be held with the open part upwards. It will be found that enough colour is thus scraped off, as it were, to charge the pen: by a similar method the drawing pen is charged.

It will be well to have a drawing pen, a pair of compasses with pen and pencil legs, a few drawing pins; a drawing board, 2 feet by 18 inches, or smaller; a T square; three set squares (one 45°, the other two 70° and 20°) and respectively 3 inches, 6 inches, and 9 inches in length. The latter will be found more practically useful than all sorts of parallel rulers; but as their use is not generally familiar to any but architectural and engineering draftsmen, it may be useful to add an explanation of it.

Having adjusted the cardboard by means of the T square on the drawing board, secure it by pins. To draw any number of parallel lines it is now merely necessary to lay the T square across the cardboard, in a direction perpendicular to that of the desired lines, taking care, of course, that the cross piece of the T is well against the edge of the drawing board, and kept firm by a weight; and then keeping one side of the set square against the side of the T, to slide it up and down as occasion shall require.

It will be found very useful both for keeping the T square steady, and for tracing and other purposes, to have a couple of small weights—lead is the best material—about the size of a child's large toy brick, or—say—3 inches long, 2 inches wide, and ½ an inch deep. Any plumber can cast them. Cover each of them with a piece of foolscap, or other paper not too smooth, folding it up like a parcel, and sealing the ends down on the upper side. The advantage of this plan is, that the envelope can be removed and renewed as it gets dirty. Handles to weights, or thick weights, are a mistake; they catch the hand.

As greater neatness and accuracy in curves are sometimes necessary than can be attained by any but the most practised hand, it will be found useful to have a few French curves; these can be procured at any artists' colour shop, or drawing instrument maker's.

Three brushes will be enough. Washing, as in water-colour drawing, being never used in illuminating, no large brushes are needed; the largest need not be more than half the size of a lead pencil, the second of course smaller, and the third a very fine one. They should be of sable; and carefully selected for firmness, compactness, even point, and absence of straggling hair.

A slab or palette for the colours, and a separate saucer or slab for Indian ink should be provided.

It will be necessary also to have an ivory point for tracing off, and a small agate for burnishing and other purposes; both are to be procured at the artists' colour shop.

Of course tracing paper will be required—the French is the best—as well as a sheet of red paper for tracing off. Red paper, though readily procurable in the artists' colour shops, and perhaps most conveniently so, is nevertheless simply and easily constructed. Any one who is desirous of making his own, has merely to take a sheet of foreign post paper, scrape a piece of red chalk over it, and then rub in with a piece of soft chamois leather or wadding, until the paper is evenly covered, not making it too thick, or it will trace off clumsy lines.

The beginner being now furnished with all necessary materials, the shortest and most comprehensible way of instructing him in the use of them, will be to take two or three of our own examples, and ask him to follow us through the process of executing them. To take a very simple one first, we will select any one of the letters in No. 3. The piece of cardboard is supposed to be laid on the drawing board, and kept steady by a single pin in the centre of its upper side, there being no need for perfect rigidity as there are no squaring or parallel lines in this illumination. Proceed to trace the initial from the example by laying a piece of tracing paper over it, with weights to steady it, the same weights may be easily so arranged as to keep the book open as well. Run over every line with your softest pencil with a fine point, and a light hand. Remove the tracing paper, and adjust it over the cardboard, so as to bring the tracing over the desired spot. Adjust the weights, slip the red paper underneath, take your ivory point and begin tracing off; and of this, let it be remarked, that nothing but practice can give the beginner the requisite skill to make a good tracing. A heavy hand, or a broad point will produce a coarse tracing; too light a hand, too faint a tracing, and too fine a point will cut through the tracing paper. It will be well to make a few trials first, and even during the progress of a tracing, especially if it be an elaborate one, to lift the lower corner of the tracing paper carefully now and then, so as not to disturb the weights, and to see that all is going on as it should. The tracing being complete, proceed next to outline it in Indian ink, with a pen. For this purpose prepare some ink in the manner already described, on its separate slab. The ink outline should be complete—strong and weak where needed, as in the outline illustration of our specimen, and should be clean and firm—all this while keep a *clean* piece of paper under the working hand.

The outline being completed, the next thing will be to prepare the colours. For either of the initial letters in Example 3, red, green, and gold are the only colours needed; and this may be the most suitable place for introducing a few words about what is technically called 'body colour.' Body colour is very largely used in all ancient illumination, whether English, French, Italian, or Oriental; but is most prominently observable in the Italian. It is obtained by simply mixing a small quantity of some opaque substance with the colour. Zinc, or Chinese white, are most commonly employed for the purpose; and the best mode of construction is to have the white in one of the metal tubes, squeeze a drop about the size of a pea on to the slab, and then rub the colour over it. Of course it will be necessary to introduce some colour a little darker than the hue desired, as the white will lighten it: thus for instance, in order to obtain an ordinary blue, it will be necessary to add a touch or two of permanent blue, or the ultramarine will turn out too pale. The advantages of body colour are twofold—first, any body colour will lie flat; next, being opaque, it can when needful be worked over other colour.

For the purposes of the illumination now under consideration then, it will merely be necessary to rub in scarlet vermillion and emerald green. Be careful to rub plenty, for it is a rule in illuminating that the colours should be laid on thick and powerful; there are no faint transparent tints, as in water-colour drawing, but even in miniature scenes, light colours are obtained not by diluting the colour with water, but by adding white to it. Another rule is, to lay on the largest body of colour first: thus in the instance before us—first put in the reds, taking care to lay on plenty of colour, to keep within the ink outline carefully, close to it but not encroaching on it, and to see that your colour lies evenly or 'flat.' Next, put in the greens, observing the same rules, and finally the gold, for it is another rule to leave the gold to the last to avoid rubbing as much as possible.

Our next example will be No. 7. Trace and outline as before. Proceed next to put in the ultramarine blues in the acanthus and flowers; next the permanent blue in the darker hues of both as well as in the initial, taking care, both in acanthus and flowers, to keep the curves clean and bold. Now colour the green leaves with emerald green, the darker lines as directed with permanent blue. The reds in the flowers follow next—all, except that in the right hand lower corner—with crimson lake, the darker hues being touched in with permanent blue, which, combining with the lake, will produce the neutral tint before referred to. The excepted corner flower will require crimson vermillion, shaded with sepia and lake. Crimson vermillion will also furnish the colour for the red flowers in the initial. Lastly, put in the golds, shading with sepia and lake.

The last Example we select is No. 9. Here, as in No. 3, proceed to trace, &c. as directed, only in this case the **T** square and set squares will come into play for the outlines of the border, both in tracing, tracing off, and in outlining —use the drawing pen for the last. The fruit, flowers, &c. must next be carefully executed with the requisite colours, according to the table given above; the gold then laid on, and afterwards the shade worked *over* the gold with a neutral tint, made of sepia and lake, as directed.

There are a few 'Tricks' which will be found generally useful to bear in mind. The agate is a useful auxiliary; with the side of it you can burnish your golds and silvers (platina) by gently rubbing them until they acquire the requisite brilliancy; and with the point of it several very pretty methods of breaking and enriching a flat gold or silver surface may be put in force, either by covering it with dots, or with dots in combination with straight or curved lines, or with a sort of Arabesque work, or—indeed, with any sort of pattern according to the designer's fancy.

Sparks of white may be with advantage introduced to throw up the edge of a leaf, or the most prominent portion of a stalk, or even to bring out the lighter edge of a letter from the background. In the latter case be careful not to obliterate the outline. The white should come just outside it, and between it and the background.

A large initial or surface of heavy colour may be very easily lightened by the introduction of a powdering of minute gold dots. These may be produced by laying on the dots, first of all, with either Chinese white, or with an article sold in the artists' colour shops, called the gold medium; and in either case touching the dots, when dry, with shell gold. The effect will be that they will stand out in strong relief from the ground on which they are laid, and will produce a very rich effect.

Finally, whilst observing the general rule to keep your work as flat as possible, be careful that it do not degenerate into tameness—rather than this—and especially with foliage, fruit, flowers, &c. do not be afraid to introduce into the deepest corners of the heaviest shades good, strong, telling touches, of almost black colour.

But above all, when in a difficulty, study the specimens enumerated above; rather err on the side of imitation than of invention.

The second point is the parallel of the first, in connexion with what may be called the manipulatory part of the treatise. Here again we must warn our readers that the book is but a Primer. The work already referred to contains no less than seven and twenty imperial octavo pages, about colours and gilding, and brushes, and other practical matters. This will furnish some idea of the magnitude of this part of the subject. But our little volume merely pretends to put beginners in the way of acquiring the power of learning more. And let us here remark, that in some particulars the colours selected, and the directions given differ, we observe, from the recommendations of other writers; and without therefore pretending for one moment to sit in judgment on those who differ with us, we will take the liberty of informing readers that our directions are based on the experience and observations of many years' extensive practice of the art in question. We may also add that, though the Primer is intended to enable beginners to teach themselves, (and if its directions are carefully attended to, will have that effect,) still it is advisable, when practicable, to carry out those directions under the eye of a master at first, even if such supervision only amount to submitting to him the results of the earlier efforts, that he may point out the secrets of any failures.

Above all, the golden rule for the student of illumination is, not to attempt too much at first. Far more real progress is made by carefully, patiently, and accurately completing a single copy of one simple letter, such for example as the N in Example No. 3, than in hurrying over half a dozen more ambitious studies, in a way which may produce a certain effect at a distance, but will not bear looking into. Like Burke, rather aim to be 'slow and elaborate,' than dashing and effective; but be industrious, and let your motto be, —"*Festina lente.*"

In conclusion, it maybe as well to impress upon the reader two points: the first is, in great part, a mere repetition of the introductory sentences of our little volume, but cannot be too repeatedly urged on his attention. There is no pretension whatever in this slight practical essay, to give anything approaching to a complete dissertation on the art of illumination; such a task would occupy a score of such volumes as ours, and be then capable of almost illimitable further expansion. We have indeed already remarked that the subject is inexhaustible; and the last notable work published on the art well observes, that 'men of the profoundest learning have devoted, some whole lives, and many of them long years, to the study of those precious pages, on the decoration of which the highest efforts of the illuminists of old were lavished; and have yet one and all confessed the partial and incomplete mastery of the subject which they, with all their labour, have been able to acquire.' It is not to be expected, therefore, that within the comparatively tiny dimensions of a Primer anything more than the merest outline was practicable, all that has been attempted then has been to furnish just such a description and dissertation as is absolutely essential to the due comprehension of what the art is, and of what it is applicable to, leaving the student to search for further information among such of the larger and more abstruse works on the subject, as may be accessible to him at the reading room of the British Museum,[13] or elsewhere. Even at the risk of being accused of repetition, it has been thought wise to impress this point strongly on the reader's attention. His motto should be an amalgamation of two well known ones—

nec temere nec timide
semper labore.

Appendix.

The following Extract from a Letter to the Editor, gives a general and comprehensive view of all the old service books, as far as illumination is concerned:—

"I think where and when the Missal came into use as an altar book, the Breviary was compiled as a Morning, Day and Evening Service-book, for use in the Quire, as well as for the private recitation of the several offices. The Gradual was to the Missal what the Antiphonary was to the Breviary. I think the main books of private devotion were the Horæ B. M. V. I do not think that the common Horæ or Hour-books, which were simply Breviaries without lessons, were ever popular, or even of much use among the laity. When the great Colbert would have a book to himself, he compiled a brief Breviary, *i. e.*, a Breviary abbreviated. Men of more unction and less sense used 'Hours of the Blessed Virgin,' and they were often, especially in the Calendar, very gorgeously illuminated. Horæ Diurnæ or Diurnales were hand-books for clerks, to say all the hours from, except matins; they were easy to carry. Indeed, my experience of illuminated books has run thus:—

> *Horæ B. M. V.*—These seem to me most numerous and elaborate in the 15th and 16th century work.

> *Evangelisteria.*—Books of Gospels next, of very much older execution.

Missalia.—Comparatively recent; rich in the Canon and Preface illuminations.

Breviaria richly and profusely illuminated are really scarce. One wonders at it; but so it is. Every now and then a handsome 15th or 16th century Breviary, commonly of French art, turns up, but not very frequently, and then not prodigally illuminated.

I have been told that some of the huge Spanish Graduals or Mass Anthem books are grandly illuminated in the way of capitals. I have seen several mutilated copies which seem to affirm the same thing."

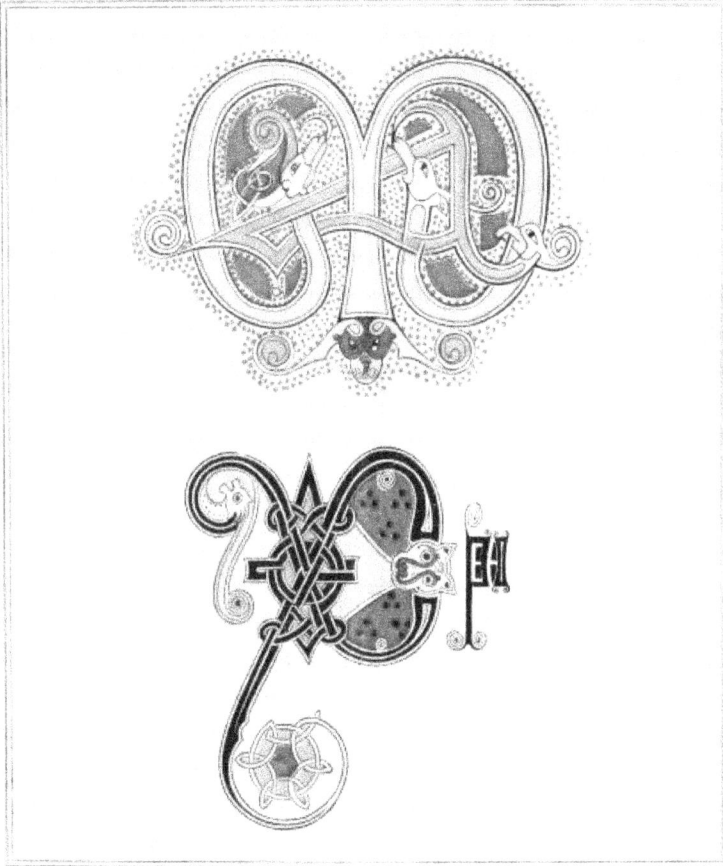

Monograms. 7th and 8th Centuries.

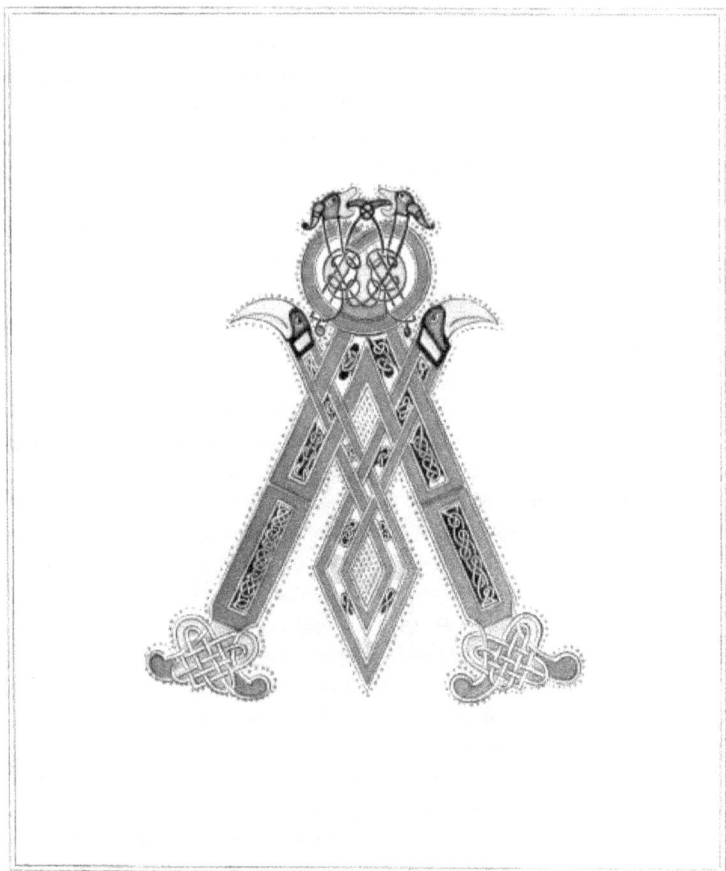

From the Bible of Charles ye Bald. 9th Century.

From a Bible. 12th Century.

Opus Anglicum.

Hours of St. Louis.

Les Merveilles du Monde. 1409.

Chronicles of England. Edward IV.

Hours of Henry VII.

Hours of Anne of Brittany.

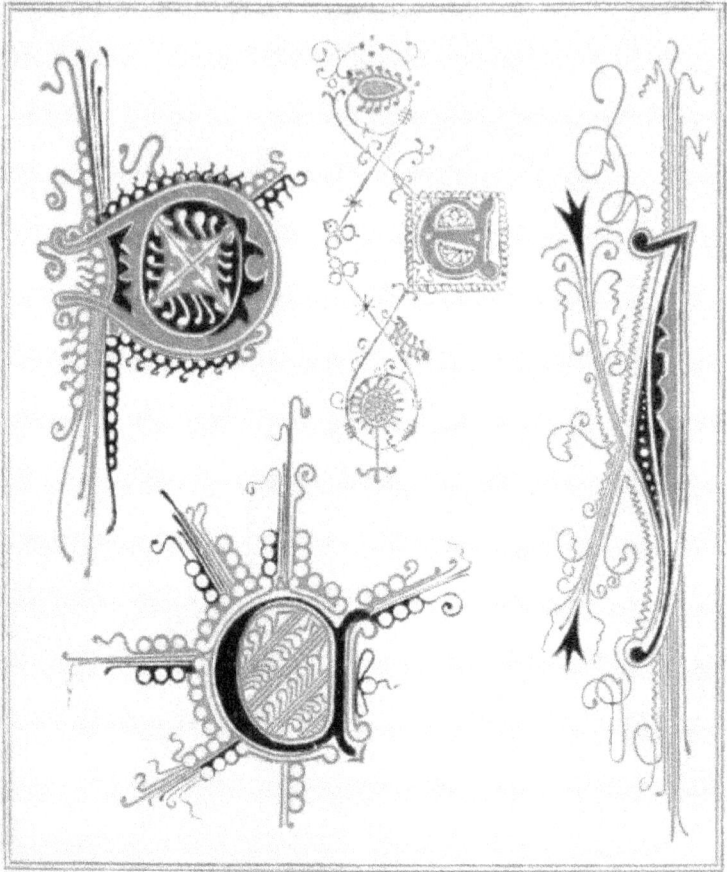

14th and 15th Centuries.

14th and 15th Centuries.

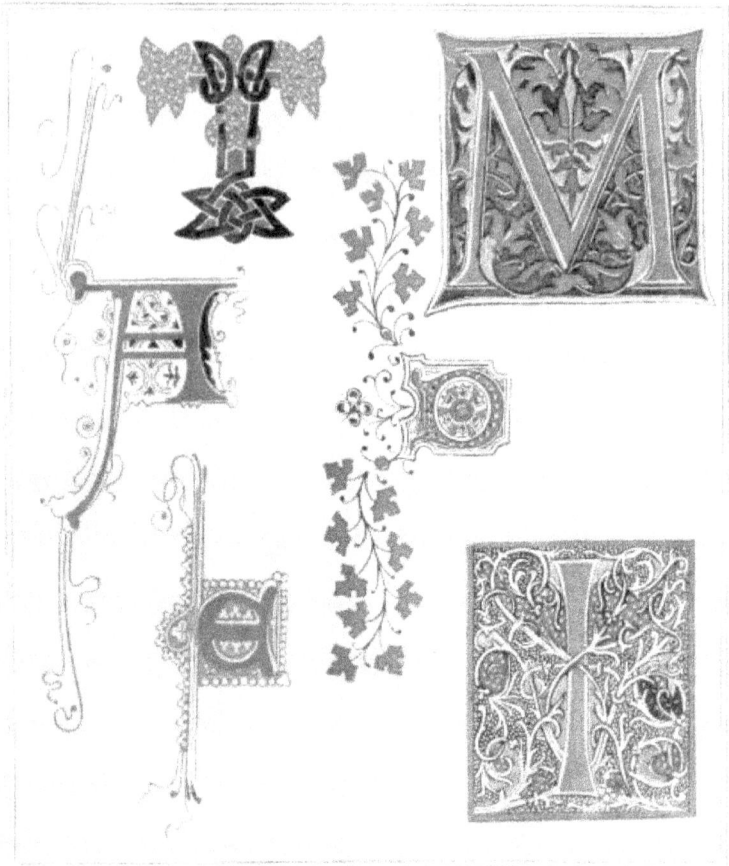

Italian and Initials. 15th and 16th Centuries.

From the Bible of Charles ye Bald. 9th Century.

From a Bible. 12th Century.

Opus Anglicum.

Hours of St. Louis.

Les Merveilles du Monde. 1409.

Chronicles of England. Edward IV.

Hours of Henry VII.

Hours of Anne of Brittany.

PRINTED IN COLOURS   BY C. WHITING, LONDON.

Just Published.

ORNAMENTAL ALPHABETS, ANCIENT AND MEDIÆVAL, FROM THE EIGHTH CENTURY, WITH NUMERALS, including Gothic, Church-Text, large and small; German, Italian, Arabesque, Initials for Illumination, &c., for the Use of Missal Painters, Illuminators, &c., &c. Drawn and Engraved by F. DELAMOTTE. Royal 8vo, oblong, cloth, post free, 4s.

"A charming little volume this is—evidently a labour of love with the artist, otherwise we should not have seen combined in its production research the most painstaking, with industry the most indefatigable. It is a book that old Lord Monboddo would have hung over, as he turned the leaves, delighted. It is designed, the title-page tells us, for carvers, masons, engravers, decorative painters, lithographers, architectural and decorative draughtsmen, and others; or, as they say in that little dry chip of Latin, almost part and parcel of our vernacular, *cum cæteris paribus*. Beyond these, however, it will hardly fail to interest the linguist, the philologist, or the grammarian. The work is, in simple truth, a curiosity. An examination of it would not have been disdained by scholars old or new, from Scaliger to Ruddiman, from Tooke to Trench, from Crichton to Mezzofanti. Yet the work is simply, as its title tells us, a book of ornamental alphabets—alphabets ancient and mediæval, from the eighth century, with numerals, Roman and Arabic. Among the letters are Gothic, Church-Text, German, Italian, Arabesque, Ornamental, and besides all these, Initials for Illumination. There are fifty pages, or rather plates, in all—each brilliantly emblazoned. The book is complete. It is the successful realization of a very happy thought, but one thus perfectly realized, through how much toil and assiduous investigation! We can very heartily commend it to the attention of those for whom it has been especially intended by its ingenious collector and designer, Mr. F. Delamotte."—*Sun.* London: E. & F. N. SPON, 16, Bucklersbury.

EXAMPLES OF MODERN ALPHABETS, PLAIN & ORNAMENTAL, including German, Old English, Saxon, Italic, Perspective, Greek, Hebrew, Court Hand, Engrossing, Tuscan, Riband, Gothic, Rustic, and Arabesque, with several Original Designs, and an Analysis of the Roman and Old English Alphabets, Large and Small, and Numerals. Collected and Engraved by F. DELAMOTTE. Royal 8vo, oblong, 4s. post free.

London: E. and F. N. SPON, 16, Bucklersbury.

DELAMOTTE'S DESIGNS FOR EMBROIDERY: Containing Initials, Emblems, Cyphers, Monograms, Ornamental Borders, Ecclesiastical Devices. Royal 8vo, oblong, in Illuminated Boards, 2s. 6d., post free.

London: E. and F. N. SPON, 16, Bucklersbury.

COUNTRY COTTAGES: a Series of Designs for an IMPROVED CLASS OF DWELLINGS FOR AGRICULTURAL LABOURERS. By JOHN VINCENT, Architect. Imperial 4to, cloth, price 12s.

London: E. and F. N. SPON, 16, Bucklersbury.

Footnotes:

[1] Single psalms, prayers, hymns, pieces of poetry, &c. written or printed with the aid of illumination, are merely representations of leaves out of books.

[2] See Appendix.

[3] There is good ground for supposing that, in Winchester, during the 11th century, there was a regular school for the art.

[4] Of the collection of the Duc de Berri we read that some of the Bibles cost 300 livres, a Cité de Dieu 200, a Livy 35, and so forth.

[5] See example No. 1.

[6] See example No. 1.

[7] See example No. 4.

[8] See fragment of Lectionary (Salisbury) British Museum, p. 27.

[9] See Examples 8 and 9.

[10] Delamotte's Book of Ornamental Alphabets will be found an exceedingly useful guide in selecting appropriate character.

[11] The Guide Book referred to has three sets of pagings: one for the King's and Grenville Library, denoted here as KL.; one for the MSS. Saloon, denoted here as MS.; the third for the Prints and Drawings.

[12] All these specimens are in the King's Library.

[13] We have, to our surprise, found so much misconception abroad on the subject, that we think it worth while to inform our lady readers that in this room there are seats specially set apart for ladies.

www.ingramcontent.com/pod-product-compliance
Lightning Source LLC
Chambersburg PA
CBHW021525270326
41930CB00008B/1096